Marriage:

a sentence

BOOKS & PAMPHLETS BY ANNE WALDMAN

On the Wing

O My Life!

Giant Night

Baby Breakdown

No Hassles

West Indies Poems

Life Notes

Self-Portrait (with Joe Brainard)

Fast Speaking Woman

Memorial Day (with Ted Berrigan)

Journals & Dreams

Sun the Blonde Out

Shaman/Shamane

Polar Ode (with Eileen Myles)

Countries

Cabin

First Baby Poems

Sphinxeries (with Denyse Du Roi)

Makeup on Empty Space

Invention (with Susan Hall)

Skin Meat Bones

The Romance Thing

Den Monde in Farbe Sehen

Blue Mosque

Tell Me About It: Poems for Painters

Helping the Dreamer: New &
    Selected Poems

Her Story (with Elizabeth Murray)

Not a Male Pseudonym

Lokapala

Fait Accompli

Troubairitz

Iovis: All Is Full of Jove

Kill or Cure

Songs of the Sons & Daughters of
    Buddha (with Andrew Schelling)

Iovis II

La Donna Che Parla Veloce

Au Lit/Holy (with Eleni Sikelianos
    & Laird Hunt)

Young Manhattan (with Bill
    Berkson)

Polemics (with Anselm Hollo &
    Jack Collom)

Homage to Allen G. (with George
    Schneeman)

Kin (with Susan Rothenberg)

One Voice in Four Parts (with
    Richard Tuttle)

Marriage: A Sentence

Marriage:

a sentence

Anne Waldman

PENGUIN POETS

PENGUIN BOOKS
Published by the Penguin Group
Penguin Putnam Inc., 375 Hudson Street,
New York, New York 10014, U.S.A.
Penguin Books Ltd, 27 Wrights Lane,
London W8 5TZ, England
Penguin Books Australia Ltd, Ringwood,
Victoria, Australia
Penguin Books Canada Ltd, 10 Alcorn Avenue,
Toronto, Ontario, Canada M4V 3B2
Penguin Books (N.Z.) Ltd, 182-190 Wairau Road,
Auckland 10, New Zealand

Penguin Books Ltd, Registered Offices:
Harmondsworth, Middlesex, England

First published in Penguin Books 2000

10 9 8 7 6 5 4 3 2 1

LIBRARY OF CONGRESS CATALOGING IN PUBLICATION DATA
Waldman, Anne, 1945–
  Marriage: A Sentence.
    p.   cm.
  ISBN 0 14 05.8922 8
    1. Married people—Poetry.   2. Marriage—Poetry.   I. Title.
  PS3573.A4215M36   2000
  811'.5421—dc21   99-046545

Printed in the United States of America
Set in Bembo
Designed by Mia Risberg

for Kristin & Alan

&

for Nick & Jerry
"made in heaven"

Grateful acknowledgment is made for permission to reprint an excerpt from "Marriage" from *The Happy Birthday of Death* by Gregory Corso. Copyright © 1960 by New Directions Publishing Corp. Reprinted by permission of New Directions Publishing Corp.

Some sections of this work which is conceived of as a "serial" poem under one rubric have been published in variant forms and earlier versions in the following magazines: *The American Poetry Review* (even keel; heuristically speaking; alien kinship; men ought to love men; rhumba; seclusion, concealment & veiling; street of human bodies; obedience & the rose; mother grace; her sure joy; common law), *Bombay Gin* (by candle's light a bedouin, blessing, climbs a tower as in a tale, dark o' night, covetous, 50 string lute), *Melancholy Breakfast,* (sexual motion, suchlike), *Napalm Health Spa* (obedience & the rose, common law), *The Poetry Project Newsletter* (tell a story about a threshold here, dark o' night, pillar of fire, on a knee, gender game, even keel, stereo), *Pharos* (ius primae noctis, china, science annals), *Prosodia* (alien kinship, says I was the Trobriand islander, Kaligat, abate the clause), *6ix* (climbs a tower as in a tale, elapidation, tell a story about a threshold here, pillar of fire), *Shiny* (flame or flaming), *Sub Voicive Poetry 1998 #12* (untitled), *Sulfur* (by candle's light a bedouin, male gaze male, heuristically speaking), *The Walrus* (wine cup of night play).

"nijinsky" derived from Nijinsky's journal. Words by William Blake in "the marriage of William Blake" from Peter Ackroyd's *Blake: A Biography*. Shamanic reference draws on Mircea Eliade.

With thanks to Cedar Sigo for attentive encouragement.

Photograph of author copyright © 1999 by Kai Sibley.

If you had three husbands.
If you had three husbands.
If you had three husbands, well not exactly that . . .
—Gertrude Stein

Should I get married? Should I be good?
Astound the neighbor next door
with my velvet suit and faustus hood?
— Gregory Corso

two by two in the ark of
the ache of it.
—Denise Levertov

CONTENTS

Marriage:

a sentence

A vision of a wifely woman one half of her face black the other half red. O sorcerer wife tell me what I am to become. I who am black & blue. I am the *ayami* of your ancestors, she says, I love you, I have no husband now you will be a consort to me & I will teach you husbandly sorcerer things. The assistant spirits are here to help you heal, she says, you are going to do this be my witchy husband & if you won't obey I'll kill you. I am terrified. I sleep with her like my own wife. She is a wife I think a wife. She lives on the mountain in a hut I stay down here. Sometimes she this wife comes to me under the aspect of an old woman, sometimes a wolf & she I think a wife is terrible to look at. Huge body. Damaged teeth. Matted hair. Sometimes she comes as a winged tiger. I mount her maw fearfully & she takes me to different countries. I see a country of wizened old men & a country of cackling old women. I see a country of young struggling arguing to be married. I see men loving men I see women loving women. I see men changing into women to love women women changing into men to love men. I see the end of lawful marriage time. She gives me the *jarga* (the panther), the *doonto* (the bear) & the *amba* (the tiger). They come to me in my dreams, large & panting. They help me in my travel in my husbandly duty. O what a wife my wifely *ayami* who makes them come to me, it is she a wife I think who speaks through my mouth, it is she the wife who inhabits my belly & the bellies of the magical animals. She who works for us & with us it is she again a powerful wife, it is she my wifely sorcerly *ayami,* a terrifying sexual motion.

— *sexual motion*

I

mystic songs
split the head
(implicit passion)
but bind all two—
of thee, nimble-footed-one
with eye of dawn, tiger tooth—
  humble consort foresworn
    whoever ye be
with me or another
    brother to brother to sister
      to lover

& mount a text toward
golden ceremony
illegal tho it be
as you mount your mate
  where spheres materialize
abode: abyss: afterimage
  no whim of angle
    initiation's mark,
      or beautiful pointillist
    scarification
lingers like painting
save respite of sex's sense
    of sentience,

of contract
half & half & half of—
  plus all married sentences

                            — *tally*

One said once an overt thing a relevant thing & the first time heard it was not "parents" it was not "couple" even, it was not even curing or a problem. Even then or even everyone seemed to live in one bed which took up a living room evenly. Suppose the marriage bed suppose it bled. The infant bows her head to ponder. A large head upon a child's intellect whose shoulder sprouts wings is hers. Winds inside a mythic winsome shoulder, hers. Wonderful to be winged in poetry, *Let me not to the marriage of true minds admit impediments.* What was a mind albeit true. Rue, hers. Ride fine bird of prey or perhaps albatross beckons you. Assuage arrange mirage forage that would be a storybook marriage. Phoenix for these married ones, *auto da fe.* Were their little rooms inside with beds in them in this one mind with eyes for windows just for pleasure & shudder? Wonder what is theirs. What does "theirs" mean? Mess through a wooden scent of pine drawer as in *don't mess around in* their drawers. Tables with humanoid legs & scent of love & mix in random familial tears. Hand & hand with marriage go blessed spring-offs. Something in this one whose nature is curious. Mysterious love instruments in another. Danger. And needles for a diabetic confused with drama with discretion at the bedside of valour. Or, you might say, a winged prickly hope. Panties from Pan, god of Panic. And was a child's imagination & pandemonium to go hand upon hand with marriage? That could be strange. Spherical bodies in the wondrous marriage bed. Jungle of sheets & pained reigning flesh. Pillows & eyes for breathing. Mating calls. A bird in the bed? Marriage is a tangible mating place surely. That it manufactures noble criterion or psalms of faith in its hardship & sober fruition is good is strange. My hands exist because of marriage, deft fingers because of marriage. Toes prehensile because of marriage. Groomed hair shiny: marriage. Caustic of head, marriage makes you that way. Because of marriage the moon rises. To come to life knees elbows ears eyes. Come to life & negotiate genetic ankles. Tongue touches roof of mouth to come to life & speech because of marriage. Something walks in cytoplasmic marriage & makes you that way. Someone walks away from cataclysmic marriage & makes you that way. Someone walks toward calm marriage & then away from are you then made a particular calm way or not? Walk up a flight & enter in a calm marriage, fly into conciliatory arms because of marriage. One lives in such a temple of love to feel restless mystical violent obsessive curious dizzy deranged hungry out of place adaptable tender timorous homespun incomplete tempestuous calm & strange of body trembling because of marriage.

— *solipsistic, anatomical*

—*my love*
—*yes*
—*woolen blanket's harsh*
—*yes*
—*love harsh too?*
—*no, gentle whether it lasteth or not*
—*old one in the quilt see her handwrought stitch*
—*ancients arriving soon*
—*is there room?*
—*you mean do we fit in there in them in the tomb with them?*

— **kinship's touch away**

One could live outside two married bodies & be or not be a financial gain. Arms are columns of fire with work to do. Roll sleeves up get down to business with work to do. Head ablaze because humans are always thinking thinking with work to do. Language is prehensile working volumes in magnified light with thought of work to do. Language on a tongue in tongue'd sequence full bloom wrought to do. Objects like swallow & tone arm collide in speaking language while labyrinths exit the mouth & young mind muses: are air & language one? And glossalalias? Gossamer, a film. One & one & one & one & one to stretch lengthen conquer & divide. Then sound the integers of hand & baby's fulcrum of identity to move the objects around the room. Shadows at night on rice paper screen tumble with traffic. Libation lights, lights for nerves to fizzle & sleep. *Sleep head* she says he whispers *sleepy a head*. Now go to sleep for tomorrow. Won't you please it's coming soon sleep is coming soon. Tomorrow you are bigger to push the objects around a room. Go to sleep for tomorrow. Animals inside the bed will help you in the task. Push the animals around a room tomorrow. Tonight they navigate without you. Animals in a head of sleep grant wishes that lions will not harm you. Birds are your friends. Elephants carry you. And dolphins. Dolphins will love & carry you. Tigers will not harm you. Sheep are gentle & will not harm you. No spiders will harm you I will not let the spiders harm you.

— *animal'd with job to do*

—contain her if you can
—for jealousy?
—she ripped the picture of her stepdaughter out of its frame
—unnerving, how natural
—what is not-kin if not unkind but turn it around
—work with the local deities they will not harm you
—you tell her they will not harm her
—[turning to her] work with the lokapalas they will not harm you

— *duo*

Say "tree" say "on the hill." Say "game" say it is "over." Say [*turning to her*] "the hand marks the seconds." Say "the hand marks the hours." Say "the horse in the harness." Say "insatiable appetite." Say "tuning fork." Say "came off the desert looking for water." Say "the messenger's narrative." Say [*turning to him*] "thirsty for home & hearth." Put your feet up take a load off. Say "marriage is always timely." Marriage was on clypsedric time. Stops one from always moving around. Are you still an umbilicus? No, a roving spirit a free agent an independent entity a marvelous conglomeration of tendencies the hairiest bag of water a water carrier a carriage trader with flute & flask before city sidewalks were wood trains run through me, hear them at night? A two-note Sally mule train Sally ghost of a fickle lover a small-time settler panning for gold with a Sally by his side. I am also the combined spoils of war. This is market time. To make a deal a fair exchange. I am a couple. This is market time. A gin fizz rupture. Psyches pitted against each other for spoils of war. I am a slave trader & she's my sex slave a party girl an old flame in transit. And to mark the time for Cold War objectives isn't marriage timely now? Musical partitions separate the girls from the wives. Jazz is her sex religion. Notes in frazzled mind. Say "radio" say "comes on a wave" say "singing voices." This is five minutes away. Say "Justice of the Peace." This is an hour. This is long. Come here. Touch me. Do you want me? For keeps? Turn over the pages in the brain. This is paper. Put it in writing, a "contractual nuptial." This is magic. This is something borrowed. This is what you can say is "god." Shift the load to the Lord. No this is something needs a Marxist blessing.

— *by candle's light a bedouin*

or/blurt
  stages/
wild mandible love

flex
  a Frenchiest kiss
blur
      love focus
not a god's
  economic viability
but strength between
legs
  astride lover's
makes
the tent
shake
O Bedouin

he has a lamp on high
  & portable chattel rigs
carries off a spoil
be she baggage woman
or no
shall travel distance/
shant?

get yr own map, woman

                    — *blessing*

Who lives with a just war honorable mail order catalog afraid to venture out on the model war friendly streets bombs burst in air. A volunteer job Brit streets done underneath the roiling it's a just honorable war street just made for war & constant war mongering & more than one hungry mouth to feed inside a shelter. War bride. Hope chest. Take shelter in the honorable war just as in justified war underground with the honorable friendly blanket. With soup cans for eyes, with a gutted-out pig, with a staunch newspaper pile and burning headlines & bundle of sticks for kindling. Across the ocean the other wife works in a tie factory all day long, long long months, paints them with a color of blood & color of idyllic green countryside. Simple yellows for yellow jacket she says like a country woman & hope a bit of sunshine. Blue for sky & hope so a bit of it, hope, she does hope he's home today maybe wait again in her handkerchief tomorrow he'll be home. Maybe a hopeful letter some news stuck in the blue metal slot.

— war bride

kiss
hand
some skull part
tongue-kiss
your tongue, skull again
 & come to me kissful
 with comely
wolf–teeth
bared in passion,
    skulk this way skull
  shake male
parts, an old vaudeville tune

come roll 'round

 animal groom
to order up
 a conjured conjugal magic
   advertises
 having
 voice
ready to howl
at a touch of
 bride let's hear

— *mail-order groom*

Moment hangs from a mouth. I love you Christ the husband but trees are grander. I love you Virgin Mary but earth is deeper. Bow down. And breath is sucked in proud & ordinary to prove that one is alive & separate & grander. Moment I am all here hold on hold on & close tangential plangent eyes. She is Queen-Iris-Eye-Lavender-of-Beauteous-Virgin-Stealth whose one praying thought is to think of little jots to praise & say to him. Say to win him in wind. Odin. Jataka Tales, the many lives of Buddha or a treatise to prove absolute gender bias in religion. Rumination. All mistakes I pledge to take them back to the holy book she says to him. Lick the motes from my eyes she says to him. Insemination. Come out from under your car hood. Moment at a tower window somewhere between heaven & earth or ground & tree who marry in bright blue air. Everything is clean up here. A grease monkey wrapped in mummy cloth. Climb into the thought of your golden bride-to-be in your duo mummy cloth. Solid at the tower window waiting for the tower of a man to prick a solid body & then you can leave me. Go now down my hair, as you might say "down the elevator." Solid moment I am all here hold on & wait for me: White Errant Knight. I'll leave spot of blood on the erratic bed sheet. You can move off now you may move on errant one. Soiled not solid his rod's down. Marriage for the lubricating bed paved with flesh. Roads. Highways. Rape. God. God could be paved with flesh. I saw a river. I saw a religious ocean. It was sex, all sex. In a book once upon a time you saw it too & it was all sex. Look down at the street all the copulations. Sex above now looking down with eager eye on the street all copulations. Streets paved with flesh. Building made of flesh and pulsing. It trembles. The tower trembles with many rapes-to-be. What century? Or rescue missions. Pulse & tremblings. Too many couplings. Answer my questions. Say "quivers." Museums with pictures of men & women in them are always questions & quivers & incarnations of peaceable married kingdoms. Invention of marvelous animals. I was a monkey & married a monkey once. Once an ox, o yes I married an ox once. Cowgirl once. Herder once. Swine.

Yes. Rouged-up faces emerge from post-coital flesh. Faces are lit-up questions & answer "yes." Sex coil quivers hold his magic arrows. Walls paved with flesh & houses are questions. Sex is hidden in the pictures. A woman lies in a bathtub Ophelialike, did she she certainly did drown for love when Bonnard took a mistress. Ceases quivering flesh, flesh. More animals in couples board Noah's ark. The marrying kind. Meticulous industry of painted coupled animals. Couples work hard to be inside the paintings. Couples work hard in their breeding sex. And what else? Sports utility vehicles. Day begins again. Moment hangs from your mouth. Open up & let me drop down to lover or else he comes to the tower bed to wed me bleed me. Heroes are always climbing up or coming home in vehicles in books. Home is up a step. One step & one step & up a step one foot at a time. And sometimes working. Say "I would like to paint." Say "I would like to paint your picture standing by a medieval tower." Close eyes see romantic pictures with spears & shields & virgins to pierce inside them. Paint a picture he's on a horse he's got a lance he's looking for a virgin smear out the eyes. Left to devices one does this & up a vertiginous step & up a step.

— climbs a tower as in a tale

13

virgin
    intacta
she is "one-in-herself"
   then wed against will

  down by the merry wood
who loves to lie with me

having
   a past is part
of marriage
in many developing countries

we don't marry, *she said*
because of economics

the fires of Kalimantan

clear away stones
to make room in each other

a hand goes
   down on him

throttle manhood's

dowry

                 — **elapidation**

The country is calling, Marry Uncle Sam. Rudimentary fear. War breeds marriage. Marriage is good for capital. R's brother brings home a Korean wife. A's sister is clear about marrying him in his uniform. Marriage is as good as a job marriage comes with a job. Or lobby in a health class wanting information on *pubis* on pubic. On contraception. It is better to marry than have sex. Completion of the circle. Some poorer pale illustration of a mythic bond and there were bows abounding, maryjanes abounding. So & so becomes stereotypical. *I want to get out of here.* When you say "fifties" what do you really mean? A movie star? As if a poodle skirt keeps your eyes on the prize. The gods on Olympus were already married, the presidents were married, the ministers were married. Jews were married, black people are married atheists are married Poles get married. Italians & Protestants especially seem to get married. The whole world is marrying. Somebody else is "queer" or strange. Sentences are sweet so & so's when they are queer with a semicolon or a torqued pluperfect tense. When will you ever not be going stronger on the clear sentence structure. Margaret Mead described a different kind of tribal ceremony & would I would have been inside a Samoan dream I might have always ever been perfectly wed. Wed to my kin, my kind whose totem is woods-related. I gather I hunt I gather I hunt. I hunted. Never for a husband.

— *tell a story about a threshold here*

though
  claimed
or spoken for
  another kin answers
    her mating call
implicit climb
from the beginning
that they would cast a flower over the village wall
  & whoever caught it was to be "wifed"
  & our headwoman would have a "vision"
inculcating fire induces fire resembles fire,
paints fire paints a clime of fire
paints her "daughter" with fire

limb-kin, kin of sweat
            night-kin, metonymy
      kin rambler,
            kin of the ox totem,
kin far to the farthest to the next-of-kin next to him
            kin that would make sense
so that our eyes stay brown
      our hair webbed of plant texture
genes don't go hog-wild in derision

                    — **pillar of fire**

In the county of Durham men with guns escort the bridal party to church. *(stop)* The guns are fired at intervals over the heads of the bride & bridesmaids. *(stop)* In Cleveland guns are fired over the heads of the newly married. *(continue)* The sedan chair in which she rides is disinfected with incense. Before the bride leaves the sedan chair the bridegroom must fire three arrows at its blinds. A mock payment is required at the door of the bride's house. *(stop)* A Taoist priest riding a tiger & brandishing a sword is painted on the front of her chair. *(continue)* I pierce the eyes of the spirits who surround the bride & touch the marriage shed with a sword three times. It's an old Roman custom where the bridegroom combs the bride's hair with a spear, a *caelibaris hasta.* Please give food (rice) to the evil influences so that they depart. *(stop).* Please (also) give food for securing all maiden fertility. Lustrations neutralise the mutual dangers of contact. Give the bride a bath of holy water. *(continue)* Fumigate the bride. Here, pour over some *tepong tawar*—neutralizing riceflower water—over her. *(stop)* In British Guiana before marriage a young man's flesh is wounded & he is sewn into a hammock full of fire ants. *(help)* The bride has to look at the sun on the day before marriage. *(aaaah)* In central Asia we greet the rising sun. The bride is conveyed in a basket. *(stop)* Among the Zulus it is against etiquette for the bridal party to enter the bridegroom's hut in the daytime. The Caucasian Republic of Ingushetia will hold a referendum on February 28, 2000, on whether to legitimize the traditional practice of letting suitors kidnap their brides. *(stop) (help) (continue)*

— *more mores*

stop: *if*
    the
    *moon goddess (*opener of the womb*)*
visits a Winnebago
    in his sleep & presents herself
in his dreams
help: *he must ever after*
    become a Cinaedi
a homosexual
continue: *he wears women's clothes,*
    performs women's tasks
& takes a husband

                 — expedition to a lake

One said once to get down on a lithesome knee & ask for a fecund hand in marriage. Rove about was only yesterday, sounds mute or a moot point talking formality today. One hundred wives in Swaziland. Its fecund aspects that get everyone down to the floor while Persian rug & details of posterity for roving drain the house. Victoria's lace a grandmother sewn off she died once & one dressed in black & one didn't wear something borrowed the first time was that an old wives' problem. Victoria's? Superstition abounds like ivy & something blue another old wife asks. Ask a Mister's permission for her hand in marriage but the handshake of the bridegroom to be he thinks is weak like a gay man like a drugged man, not the Earthy Fecund Man. Could be. Asks for assurance, knees & hands. Ho. Hard to please in the cool modernist New York springtime. Mister & me. We were very gay then.

— *on a knee*

one said
  once
get
  down
upon a
  knee

will
    take
the girl
as she
stands
    down

  & her wobble
  for
the
world
does
bend the mind
  up
in obliged
supplication
  of hand

whatever else
they may
think,
    hand
over heels
over
    mouth

knee shaky
　　in atonement
　　　nails
—*paint them*—
　　　　ruby red

　　　　　　　　　　　— *gender game*

Power to the all men all women all people. Solidarity against a mutable war. Up all night plots a next reponse, teach-in, or break the laws. Horrors of the Nam. Keep posted. More souls shipped off yesterday. You might jog down St. Mark's Place then turn a corner to the churchyard where one could always & did set a mouse free in & he becomes a churchmouse shy hiding. Pain in the rafters ghost chains from the memory of slave pews stiff upright boards, not a place you could slouch get comfortable in because when you say marriage one's thinking wedding which is in a house of the Lord even if the bridegroom to be is Jewish. How they were treated then & now. Ghost chains. Slave souls to save. Slaves in the house of the Lord a contradiction it's the masters need saving. He & she take an oath to poetry's historical imperative. Petrus Stuyvesant also haunts about with a pegleg. There are canonical stories. Obetrol is a speed pill you take to get your gumption up. It takes its toll the world intensified by this mutual-bond-plan. You are inextricably linked to the powers of your city. You wanted to have a party. You are bound to the financial difficulties of Herman Melville several blocks away. The father-in-law disappears & goes on a bender invoking Ho Chi Minh long may he win he sobs, he who fought an honorable war. Sobs because the daughter will be held apart & one generation replaces another. Never make the mistakes *I* made, never marry *too* young. Never send your children to war. Held aloft perhaps but never apart. On a pedestal. She will never be a single but still a daughter & how would he ever give her away. Not really. Deny that gesture in blue. What I was hoping was an oath to be friends perhaps til death do us part. Mister, Mister. It wants to be true. Up the aisle with you.

— *Herman & Ho*

brassy choir lament
  never
humble suit
   I tender
a friend speaks

no, I do]   [no, I do

nerve's perception
   thru saintly
stain glass
  monster mister
 glint be fashioned
to keep the cult utensils safe from harm

  time's radiant valley
tho
I walk thru death's shadow
   demur

valley's pride a vale
medieval strain
  to be melting girl
& beauteous
in woven veil
   or psalm duress
or
old-fashioned
   the act pierces me,
I am slain
 so many of our boys
overseas
  we

take pity on their escalating pain
      & that of people
they bomb
      to pronounce you
man & wife

                          — rite

Marriage marriage is like you say everything everything in stereo stereo fall fall on the bed bed at dawn dawn because you work work all night. Night is an apartment. Meant to be marriage. Marriage is an apartment & meant people people come in in because when when you marry marry chances are there will be edibles edibles to eat at tables tables in the house. House will be the apartment which is night night. There there will be a bed bed & an extra bed bed a clean sheet sheet sheet or two two for guests guests one extra towel. Extra towel. How will you be welcomed? There will be drinks drinks galore galore brought by armies of guests guests casks casks of liquors liquors & brandies brandies elixirs sweet & bitter bitter bottle of Merlot Merlot Bustelo coffee. Will you have some when I offer. When you are married married there will be handsome gifts for the kitchen kitchen sometimes two of every thing. Everything is brand brand new new. Espresso coffee cups, a Finnish plate, a clock, a doormat, pieces of Art. And books of astonishing Medical Science with pictures. Even richer lexicons. When you are married married there will be more sheets sheets & towels towels arriving arriving & often often a pet pet or two two. You definitely need a telephone & a cell phone when you are married married. Two two two two lines lines lines lines. You need need separate separate electronicmail electronicmail accounts accounts. When you are married married you will have sets sets of things things, of more sheets & towels matching, you will have duplicates of things, you will have just one tablecloth. When you are married married you will be responsible when neighbors neighbors greet you. You will smile smile in unison unison or you might say he is fine, she is fine, o she is just down with a cold, o he is consoling a weary traveler just now, arrived from across the Plains. She my husband is due home soon, he my wife is busy at the moment, my husband he is very very busy busy at the moment moment this very moment. Meant good-bye, good-bye. When you are married married sex sex will happen happen without delay delay. You will have a mailbox mailbox & a doorbell doorbell. Bell bell ring ring it rings rings again a double time. You do not have to answer. That's sure for when you are married people people understand understand you do not not have to answer answer a doorbell doorbell because sex sex may happen happen without delay delay. You will hear everything twice, through your ears & the ears of the other. Her or him as a case case may be be. He & he & she & she as a case case may be may be. When you are married married you can play play with names names & re-name yourself if you like. You can add a name, have a double name with a hyphen if you like. You can open joint accounts when you are married. Marriage is no guarantee against depression. A shun is no guarantee against anything. Marriage is no guarantee against resolu-tion. Revolution is a tricky word word. Here, you hear here? Mar-riage is sweeter sweeter than you think. Think.

— *stereo*

ornamental
presence
  sculpted

  ivory irony
or virgin flesh

Pygmalion & Galatea
tell a tale
he gives the
    statue kisses
courts with flatteries
dresses
    in fine clothes
lies her
  on a purple bedizened couch

o partner of my bed! he cries
the gods grant me!
& Venus's altar
blazes
    three times
& any goddess knows what he means
growing warm
    the wax girl

                              — wax girl

I loved him on the sofa. I loved him on the floor. I loved him from the window from sitting on the windowsill watching him out the window. I loved him in the afternoon of the afternoon before the time we just got out of bed. Loved him the afternoon they announced the bombing & we just got out of bed & went to resist. Sometimes we traveled & resisted and one could be "Mrs" & traveling you weren't just wearing a gold band to keep the men from following you you were wearing a gold band because it had been placed on the hand that was asked in marriage. In Italy the hand went to sleep in a thousand golden places. The hand placed an offering on several marble tombs. What is love said the hand that touched a thousand golden places. Love of art of beauty of a thousand golden places. I put my other hand through the glass window not the marriage hand. There was a picture of the Pope on the hospital wall. Crown him with a thousand golden sunrays with staff. He was not exactly comforting more than that he was exacting in a thousand naked places. The husband collapsed in my own blood. How was that for a pagan rite? Weak in the knees. We were smart enough to make a tourniquet. There was a crucifix on the other hospital wall. A president on another, the Catholic one. One who was deciding to bomb. These are precipitous times. What is love in a thousand golden bombed-out places. But that is another story and wasn't meant to be suicidal, that story. That story was evidence that there is no guarantee in marriage against an act of violence. We certainly know that. But an act of violence may bring a couple closer together some say. It did. It didn't. It did it didn't. Who can be sure. Did it. Undercurrent of tension is seeing all the wires in the walls on lysergic acid diethylamide which were the veins & arteries in which blood coursed through a pagan hand & wrist not the marriage hand. But look at the finger a ring once ringed in a thousand golden circles. Look at it now. Here, this finger still exists.

— *act of violence*

beauty is set apart
o beauty's cruelty set apart
   how could that be cruel
to be unalterable
   purpose apart
how passion toked
that it be done by his deft hand
  broken
the magnetic poles
  shift
in the little hut
in a wattle hymen-hut
that it is said as easily
   as cool reflection
  of heavenly bodies
said: orb for sale
 a heavenly body
all my celestial wares
    for sale

grind in
  purpose
of blessed ownership
a hand writes this down
"apart" "apart"

head spins in the tiny hut
how choices are made

voice in a
  lustral mind
arms reach up
  to hold his panting mind

she says
perfunctorily now
you took my
  maidenhead
the little
  crown
you took

— *moon-in-hand*

It was a grandmother's working class gold band & later when one wore an engagement ring made of the diamond tears of two Victorian earrings round two which came from the future mother-in-law you could say I am married to my aristocratic mother-in-law & my Christ Science grandmother. Domination of the matrix-world. Normal situations plus times of crisis make us whimper make us weep make us fools & I am in love with the old wise ladies & that's because a lineage is like a ring or a message & an interpretation. A lesson is useful here. England is coming into its own centuries ago now she's been emasculated just as she a mere woman not a country does come into her own now in her female workplace of power. Is the Church of England in crisis? I'd bet but Time is a maternal spiral. Would my finger was a peace-mission-tower bedecked with jewels I love, sparkling mountain of gems you could climb to for relief you could climb to in hope of World Peace. I'd bet if I wore them just so on my head like a crowned priest or stood upon them as conqueror to rocky peak the men I desire will have covetous dreams about me which will include the grandmother the mother & the mother-in-law & their residual religions plus a ceremony or two. Then one dark night the actual mother had her actual wedding band stolen inside the old mahogany house. Someone unnatural intruded late at night & stole it from a miniscule drawer. Later for a second ring a fake a cheap a nonhistorical ring she would be mugged in the urban setting. So people will become thieves to surrogate-marry even if a junkie is simply hungry.

— *covet*

lifetimes
   continue
tailspin
fine thread-of-poems-spin
   recount
   the trials of this & that
that the landscape recede
      before calamity
      of one nation existing
            inside another
not wanting to be there
tacit agreement not to bolt
         before
actual Nationhood arrives
my boundaries not the boundaries of
         my neighbor tho I marry him, my neighbor

enter any random brutality
 corpses uncovered at dawn
he searches for his wife
 (she had a blue dress on mottled scarf
kin to the "enemy")
rings melted down
 for gold
they say the shark people spin
      spin
just like nimble killers
   on land

                        — 50-string lute

A divinity goes mute goes charioteering goes hidden underground worshipped only in caves on the dark side in darkness of the dark side of moon. Nuanced. With her trouble in mind. With her plenty o'nuttin-trouble in mind. If it's the dark side she's after she's gone under it's bound to be an antechamber to the cavern named Blue Bride Heaven. With a switch in hand with a trail to blaze. But in water well she'll be well-dressed well-tuned with a cistern on her back an alimony paycheck with a dust broom with an eye on the back pages. You know those old sacrificial *cenotes?* She's thrown in with the other shark people & has to be back by holy Groundhog Day. A problem. And what do they do about swimming down there mucking about with the other sacrificial victims in certain cold blue death. That the murky world could exist *a priori* her long delay, that substance abuse is not a problem, that the right party will win & art & science will wed in decalcified day is not necessarily a scenario. A shrine is erected to grant immunity to kinship relations. And she will be on it burning like the incense you give a passing thought to.

— *shark people*

ask those
  who
pass
of life
a Linear B

of death
  & passing fame
& fortune
  a linear A
or common tune B

    then common risks unmediated
        induce
a brink of x chromosome
plus workaholic gloom
&
    marries one
  to the talking mirror
      of "self"
              tangential mìse en scène

a one
but common mate
  is also a raw or lawful mate
  a raw love to accomodate
        in vegetation ceremonies
with commodities
    & sweets of late
            of love
& distant mandible lore

                    — *common tune*

34

A next incredulous time o belly time was again another being blessed & another husband & already blessed with a baby in belly. Shotgun husband belly time. Then. Another round but with a baby blessed with a baby then & warm love & love him still & then then & now. Still & now & then. But under another roof another roof. Marriage is a family. Under many eaves. Doorways. Marriage is more ways to be wedded to a baby under many guises. Taking a vow to this man & baby-man many lifetimes. Marriage to the sound of a poet's harmonium and *Prajna paramita sutra*. Cupid's day. A rosy day with gusts of snow. Roses a blessing disguised as a blessing from the Tibetan lama. All's well in the rosy red belly. And he is inside me a rose is blooming. Marriage is a shotgun blessing. Marriage made blooming shotgun sense. And marriage could survive cabin fever floods icy roads separation late-night work shifts long-distance travel hospitalizations shotguns & motherhood, a paragraph. Marriage could survive ruses. And then marriage couldn't. Never use the word "divorce" it is not in the vocabulary of blessed baby belly love. And husbands become saints & brothers & fathers. Never impediments. But increments to loving paragraphs, staunch architectures of love.

— *gestational*

unless
    chromosomal
  but if . . .
cytoplasmic
 gestation
    leases a war
was
 relief illud tempus
  a babe a sentence
 inside an abode
a body
 married
to embryo
 genomic kin's
   bond a boost

mine all mine
  but mine & husband's

to burst

                    — ***gamete***

Common law you are always on your waking alarm by communal bedside's toes. Secular power keeps you on your secular toes unblessed by holy power a patriarch's hold. A woman & a woman keep the same sex faith. Others do. What's the power in common law on common ground you step upon on tiptoe. A man & a man do. Common faith. Conjugal rights for a woman & a woman will do. It is the tipped hallowed affair bold in day or was once a way to break away & went along in time became a bed a stage a blame a frame a claim a state of mind a crush some years some grounds for suit a random urge an undeniable passion never stopped went on was chimed in met the family became a family chimed in on family extended the metaphor family raised a religious family was raised beyond doubt beyond family couldn't get the sanction by day raised up a sleeve travelled through need came alive unravelled unrivaled that need came apart came to law was accepted by law downed then rounded out by law needed law need rights need common ground to fence in the communal things don't fence the trickster inside the common law inside the secular metaphor common ground in. We had it in common. But were never common. We were never random. We were in a genital conjugal situation seven years seven tides seven hurricanes seven wars seven reasons why seven simultaneities seven bold maids a milking on your guard. Common law is a right not rite. It is for every danger. Common law begs to differ. Common law sings for its supper. Common law is fine. Common law is not quite marriage. On your guard. Common law is fine.

— *common law*

guard

  up

the sleeve

  then rest unguarded

head in a hallow'd
hold of her

  he does &
then he doesn't
    love the other man

then does he rest
he does
& she?
she does rest

              — sleeve of care

How many colors in a love drama sleeping. Mauve? Tangential? Rudimentary hands held accountable. No nonsense hands that work the land but tapered fingers tipped to a sigh she notices. Handsome youth that would be hers she notices. She spots him in the schoolyard. They marry young face to belly full moon a justice just down the road but beyond a border. They will face the world together hailing hauling vicissitudes & the like. Up against a difficult country a difficult province a difficult hometown he is a rude mechanic while she drops out. There's a factory in the story, a factotem. Him. Robbery. Abortion. Car wreck. Angry mob. Lynching kind of mob. Serious face angled in light of sex with flush toward day. He's dark. What day is mauve is essential. "Our first." He has the chiseled features of a movie star. Her name is Faith. Mixed marriage. A bright one with lattice & trim. Eyes edge to window colors of skin no longer sleeping. Rouged over or rousing. Boyish & blushing of course & aroused. A checked Mexican gateway a matter of stolen identity a coverlet with dried blood. Paint it well or make the film spill their story. Faith & her man. There's a prison coming down the line. Swatches of yellow & gray. Don't run them out of town. On bed or floor poised. Poised & green when they told her she had Chinese skin was a go ahead for a mixed marriage. Thinking repose is color in the mix but no color is color without repose & a roof is a color a place to hide a meal in a color a place for a mixed marriage baby. Rest in the color of mixed minds & you won't admit impediments. Mottled skin in repose. New prisoner. He walks in. She wants her sex back in a face painted not tangible or tinged by skin but in response so that the Eros she sees is not thought back through body but held in a thought that would be her own that she acted thus & so. She wants her sex back. This was her story & she chose her man. Then an older one a cruel & managing one gets whatever he wants you've seen him in a hundred overweight movies appears to test Faith's faith. He's large & has money & he wants her & does succeed through emotional back-alley blackmail. Check it out. She wonders perforce sits in her room. She passes for light. She thinks of paint held tinged by skin that is a saintly original thing when they were young & younger the original couple she moans about after she's had sex with the intruder who says he will save her. A cynical laugh. She remembers a faraway time that they played together & would leave home & love in a car. It starts with love in a car. A prism (his) on dash reflects a thousand pricks of light over her taut breasts he's sucking. A crucifix (hers) dangling over his handsome Aztec face as love in an old Ford car a marriage enacts. She cries she would lick that thigh & taste oil & salt of her lover's prick & lick his scars through crying she wants him back it back them back never do he won't no he won't cry as I do she says because he's tough. Pink a one & pick a one green or grown fonder aqua tint the sight of breast in repose old housecoat rouged nipple that does not ask a sigh. Never hardened in prison paint.

— *nipple that does not ask a sigh*

holy family
in animal parts
    perform
bend
buckle
or
rise
    stir
or wave cult wands
then undulate
    in chain-gang caravan
    gone down
        unknown
upon one
    another's
    lap or
lanky braceletted
    shank
now revive

(predatory in paint)

hidden chamber/ceremonious bower/secret mirror/saintly costume/moorish
gait/untuned buckle/restitution of mores/costumed gent/nuptial gown/cross-
dressed damsels/cross-gendered animals/eye dilation/sweat secretion

— **predatory**

When you have amassed the tones-of-wear, of weight lift, a public life, overdrive, you are the tomes of breath & pause. *(pause)* When you are in the spirit that is dyed the color of maple leaf you are home-free. When you are in your marriage that is a love-cage that is a bond that is a way to travel heavy but you want to travel light you are in fragments. You are a woman in need of a wand in need of an ancient city. Rome is almost ready. Paris would have you. Prague, Budapest? Calcutta is a long shot. Vienna beckons. *(pause)* Cincinatti trembles. A Celtic town? Carry cans of food upstairs. Obligatory rounds of day of night. Lost illusion that could be governed by circumstance when you are married. A small staircase makes sense. The stove makes sense. A cork on the floor. Clamour weeks for sign-up-a-head-of-time & now it is free speech time. Speak up. Economic viability or ironic sensibility sets in. Laugh your head off. Salute the other. Say out loud "down the lights." *(pause)* Someone is always responding to the lantern to the libertine debt. To linoleum. A cost got figured in the way you turn a page. Very good at that. Very very good at that. You are writing the tome of Bondage, the innoculations of the tribe. He is a taboo, then she is. Allergy of someone under thirty leagues. They hide when the sirens sound. And sounding the syllables. He said "vocables." Lights on or off my friends. You can come out now. *(pause)* Two women get married to show the world they can. They adopt a daughter. Two mommies a wicked sensibility. Two mommies a sentence. On or off. On or off my friends my friends. Plans are made, dressing up for the Beltane festival. Closer in the small bed.

— *wine cup of night play*

—*a sacred marriage*
—*sex slaves in the temple that's all*
—*but singing & dancing*
—*was Sappho?*
—*Viva La Virgen!*
—*sophisticated arbitrariness*
—*tending the butter lamps*
—*syncronous/ruptured, & then a veil*
—*she holds her own*
—*mere child's game inside a marble box*
—*premium on probity I beg to differ*
—*a family lineage perhaps?*
—*deeply absorbed*
—*come round out the daughter*
—*& into inner sanctum peep*

— **hieros gamos**

Close ties both sides unless you are orphan-born. And even then &
even then & even then even if you are never even. And even then a
preparation is suitable is loving is invincible. You are a cherished trea-
sure. As orphan greet the day like any other, the one you are, the day
you are. When you are an orphan you will want all love. You might
have all love. You have that. Love. An orphan will save a marriage not
always the other way around. An orphan is mysterious. And adopts
you. An orphan is more than a heart made of red velvet. An orphan
nudges against night. An orphan strives to get through the day with-
out mistakes. An orphan dusts the house (fairy dust) without mistakes.
Never banish the orphan. Take her in.

— orphan

potency
   is not
a sacerdotal figure
   in this
revision
  acted out alone
upon a
  crazy Baptist town
    (staid?)
Bob & Mister Amorous
  won't regulate sexuality
larynx of the orphan
    or kick-ass generosity
  but set up shop together
take a vow

            — outed for eternity

Mother-in-law is absolute tyrannical law is dietary law is the vittles on the table law. Law of any land a mother claims a sentence. Or motherhood mar her paragraph. We could be in Italy. We could be in Ireland. Love, a penance. Marriage a transience. Nuances of every gesture accompany your child-borne mood. Nuances are odd & prepared to you by tyranny's food. Buy her humor being store bought. When she was an old country handmaiden she could make those dumplings by hand. Before she was a new country librarian she would have time on her kitchen hands. When you are married words at an inlawed table become weightier nuance. Outlawed you are out on the street again in Bulgaria. In Poland. In Russia. In Buchenwald. And resist being eaten. You bite on words you chew on them you spit them out you sort them out you exile them from the kitchen. You ransom them for holidays. And sing around the holidays extolling the virtues of ceremonial food. You will eat that blessed cracker. Or wreath of chilli. You will you will. A child will ask questions. You will pray at a table for the rain to fall for the ship to come in. We are thankful for this inter-married food the work of many beings & the suffering of other forms of life.

— mother grace

pass
ethos, an essay

  ethnic unleavened cracker
pass over
  days   seasons
        a month   years
  twilight
at table, the gay couple

pass the perpetual
     sugar
  inexhaustibly set at table
        a century
           in delicate Etruscan bowl

it will not harm you

— *lineage*

In some places a woman would marry a woman which torques the definition of marriage would it be so simple any such definition. For they throw stones at you in the torqued definition of marriage. It hurts to be unkind they say & cast a stone. Or someone had a man take a slug at her on an emotional national holiday because she was a known lover of woman who had a wife. And it was a man's holiday, a memorial day for dead warriors who are mostly especially in the two wars men. Or maybe she the woman slugged was a wife. This is a two wives tale. It was unseemly to see two women kissing, two women embrace under the primrose tree. Two women in a Lautrec brothel holding the tide together against the slings of men. Caressing against the tide of pimps & other men. Some get murderous in Oregon to see the women, two, shopping together as might a man & wife. Living as do a man & wife in an ordinary man & wife apartment, doing man & wife things. Except at night in the deep dark of night, they said, they who were murderous & dark. What do they do at night? While we are doing our man & wife things, what do they do in the dark of night what do they do?

— dark o' night

sleep: violent
church: receptor blocked
make love: hippocampus
work: no memory
bicker: memory
gossip: you tell me
breed: have bred will breed
drive: drive
shop: all the brittle streets
repress: dopamine
a dreadful dream: men in skirts
impose: holy evolution
destruction: all around
consumption: cells of a nutritive cycle of animal
            (eats plastic, metal etcetera)

*— **murderous man & wife things***

Whose whose property property is whose whose in the origin origin of marriage marriage. In in the the not not always always but sometimes sometimes gloom & doom gloom & doom of marriage marriage. Would would a person person buy buy another another. Could could a person person buy buy another another arrange arrange another another & be another's another's sometime sometime body body captor captor. When Diego held the paintbrushes? A rapture maybe. Mister Mister. A rupture. And make it a bond for arrangement of the other's mind & body parts. Hearts. Mrs. Mrs. Soul-rupture. And black market organs organs. And sexual psyche. Might be. Could another buy another in such a way as to own a sexual soul psyche. You who are a buying kind tell me. Joint accounts are a trusting way to go some think others are burned in the shopping spree of broad daylight. And if if separation separation sets sets in in beware beware the turning turning tide tide. Start labelling. This this is mine mine no no this this is mine mine. The child is mine. This this is surely surely mine mine. I don't think so it used to be mine mine before you were mine mine. You were never a goldmine you might add although you were mine. Things things mount up up to chastise you in their frenzy frenzy. Custody custody is brutal brutal. (*one voice*) Custody is brutal.

— *shopping spree*

—what shall I give you then?
—a child
—an interpretation of twig of bone
—libations lustrations
—holy cow coin of Mohenjo-daro
—a ring
—a sign
—a theory
—the role of widow/widower

*— **dowry***

I danced very little because I was sad & sad because I thought that my wife did not love me. I got engaged in Rio I married suddenly. I met her on the steamer *Avon*. I must say I married without thinking of the future. We spent money which I had saved with great difficulty. I gave her roses at five francs each I brought her twenty to thirty of these roses a day. I liked giving them to her as I felt flowers & understood that my love is white not red. Red roses frighten me. They come & go. Red like lovers. They wilt & die like lovers. They turn against you. They are beautiful. They are heavy in their beauty. They suck you in. They bleed. Their petals lie like corpses on the stage. White roses are a gesture & they die without a fuss. I am no coward. I married. I felt everlasting & not sensual love. I loved her passionately & gave her all I could. She loved me it seemed to me she was happy. For the first time I felt grieved three or five days after my wedding. I asked my wife to learn to dance because dancing was the highest thing in life for me. I wanted to teach her. I never taught anyone my art I wanted it for myself but I wanted to teach her the real art of dance but she got frightened. Did she no longer trust me? I wept & wept bitterly & already felt death. Had I put myself into the arms of a person who did not love me? I weep weep she weeps & weeps.

— *Nijinsky*

unsuited
& was
a root
of domestic turmoil

   (Coleridge?) (opium?)

  insularity

staring at itself

 mad eyes

needs
a separate life
  craves it

Parvati & Shiva: the destruction of the world

— *wanderlust*

It was to be a day to old flames a day dedicated to the flaming of way old old flames how they flamed in the affairs of state & held a forum of flame which is to say topics heated & argued. Flame on. Protest this love. Keep it going. An eternal flame for the martyred soldier. For the masters of the wedded universe. For heroes & heroines of field & court. For T and Erin & M & M & N & B. For L & Jill & R & J & S & Z & Y & C & F & D & E. And for O & for the other J & A. For the other L called Lucian & the other C. For difficult K and D in Thailand. For the lost explorer who wed the amorous lady astronaut. Those passionate or extinguished those driven to enormous ends of tether. For the eternal discus thower & whether to strike first forever debated & argued. For the female champ. For the players on the field all figures coming & going. We argued. We did & wedded. We did never argue. What is defeat for a lover? For a soldier? For old flame? We arranged the rooms in a domestic arrangement of claimants that precludes but doesn't exclude the live-in arrangement with an old flame. How lit up it gets the one mysterious room of dark paint with its threatening cult objects. And a corporal stares out with his World War uniform on. We as pronoun except for her rage never existed. Ex. Ex Libris. Exterminate. Extra terrestrial. Expound. Ex as a middle name. Ex are women. Ex are cults. Anger at the center at the knot in her ex heart. Forgive as if never heard from again a kind telegraphic suicide. For the boundary crossed was held in the good ex sense in rooms she would always still inhabit & everywhere as if ex windows look in on her are seen the implements of ex rage in a tight knot, still. Still waiting flaming & ready in action to be so that a step over the threshold means war. Don't cross me in her exegesis of her ex'd flame which is salvation for her exed out of here.

— flame or flaming

be
fruitful
multi-
　ply

ply earth
　have dominion

Adam found
　no help
　'mongst animals
fit for him to ply

then Lilith an artist
　comes in
then the she-serpent
then enters Eve

o justify my creation
& breed
　a little irony

— **hex**

Marry that ye may prosper & conceive a better way to be innoculated than what is left to dreamers & heads of state. So & so & her husband get this way in a kind of medicinal attraction & rejection game. Headline news. Get out coins & divination sticks. Toss for loss for toss of vestigial love. Consult the I Ching. Tarot. The ubiquitous stars. Toss for replication of desire. One seeks another to be a shadow of one's desire so that one can't get off the hook off dead meat's hot wheel without consultation confirmation predictions & what does it come in it comes in many sizes that wheel. Project the "other" *you* to be that bride that groom roles playing for eternity across wounded galaxies. And the sum is again, again, doing it again again that ye may prosper in orphan planets' other solar systems again again if the form be true. One & one. One & one. And if you are a movie star if you are a senator if you are a software dynasty if you are base lead rising to gold if you are an assassin you are listening to the doppelgangers & their virtual marriages where economies clash by night & yet you prosper you grow.

— doppelganger flame

red ray death
whips Perceval must shun
wisp
a loss we shun
we a chapel a tipsy vessel
we a fleet of couples fleeting
a motif we shun
religious persecution
shadow's opposite
we a couple a conspiracy
buried alchemy in our sweet conjunct
influence of the planets on this union
infiltrate
pisces / gemini
scorpio / scorpio
aries / libra
   aquarius / saggitarius
leo / pisces
    libra / libra
the bull / the scales
the ram / the archer
the goat / the ram
the scales / the mad twins
infiltrate virgo / virgo
capricorn / leo cancer / virgo
    the scorpion / the sting
animal'd in eternity
aries /
the lion the . . .
& etcetera
ad *rudimentary subatomic* infinitum

             — astrology a middle name

In a wealth of nations speech it goes without saying manifest destiny & promise of cattle & such. Land forms will rock you. Chattel & such. Such fortuitous peace such labor for prosperity such womanly pluck. Her photo's got sunburn & a stern command. On the map. Although a man is evidently in charge & draws it. And some mountains & some valleys to evidently cross your path. And some deserts to cross. And plains. You are a mere roadweary seedling. Takes a rest. And suchlike wheat & suchlike corn & other growing things from promised land will o'er take you. Soy, for example a bountiful crop. But more with fertilizing the meek & many animals. You need a mule train. You need sun shades. You need a heap of potatoes & meatloaf. Or meaning creative in the sense of husbanding an amendment or passing a tough resolution a sweet vision to be fulfilled among the planet's interdisciplinary mode. Goes without saying that by being husbanded you will produce. And travel. And stake a claim for breeders. The world is too much with us breeding late & soon. Suggests fertile, suggests hard work & staying in power. Do I husband you? May a woman do such. Will she lie back on the barnyard ground rich with hay & be husbanded. You mean branded as in cattle do you do you do you you do mean owned. Fucked in sweat of labor & manifest destiny. Goes with a song out on the homey range to test courage suggest courage she needs it under the hot sun facing a paternalistic non-Sufi wind. Dust moat in her maverick I told you so eye.

— *suchlike*

breach
  in the breath day

she

  maketh the
country rich

delivereth a quota
  & full of band waves

  she's my gal

hussy is her brand

I've got a mule & her name is Sal
Sixteen years on the Erie Canal
she's a good old worker
she's a good old pal

— *worker song*

Men ought to love men & do he said I thought he said no he wrote this in poetry, in a controversial poem, he said men ought to be connected ought to love men out in the open some rights please & they do of course. This was in the halcyon sixties. He said I think they do they do love one another & it was always going on (*gimme a break* my friend said he's very gay-vocal) he meant I think that's what he said men ought to love men. Ought & do, ought & do too. Moral imperative & it's true here's proof. How far we've come he said. But the (also) political woman who was also the courageous poet outspoke & took offense at such a sneer on women. She got rigid as she got older. Why put one sex down over another said over another o *gimme a break* they've got holy households, they're tying the knot in Hawai'i, they're getting rights its gonna be law its gonna be over for us the minority of whites & straights o hallelujah hallelujah praise the gay lord the gay lordy praise her name.

— *"men ought to love men/(And do)"*

touch him
  like a priest

a sacrament
learning the idea of sex change from the moon

Attis was about to wed the king's daughter
when his mother who was in love with him
struck him mad

O Attis

in ecstasy he castrated himself before the great
goddess
& in front of Cybele men become Galloi
sacrificing virility completely

— dies sanguinis

Meant to be proud meant to be astonished & full of surprise at the mere winking of flattery's sexual eye meant to be inexhaustible at the front range or outermost perimeters of underclass meant to be insurmountable meaning you couldn't climb on top of me with britches on meant a display meant a horror of violence meant destabilizing the economy downsizing wherever it is you want to stand for or on someone else's abundant shadow meant realizing the heart's always on a preternatural sleeve meant it glows in the dark meant it's mine but meant for you meant radiation counts for all that means you are about to be homeless it's a split hair way if you fight like that the system & all dear hubby meant a way out when you were needy meant slumming when you needed me meant driving home a wifey point about environmentally sound architecture meant the storm would not abate that the hurricane would cost many lives that life is not cheap though some say so who are at war let's eject them out the human kingdom the animal kingdom the kingdom of beauty & parity & divorce them from their home & that small organism the kingdom of languages & their extensive extended families meant originally trying her on for size meant he got down on his knees at last in a kind supplication for nuptial vow meant it could last it might last could it last could it possibly last & were they to breed & how many more does the coupling planet hold & were it to last would it really last & have meant something does last in the name of Allah, how many billions a planet can hold as the residue on the sleeve lasts chanting I do I do I do I do I do I do I do I do I do I do I do I do do I & I do lasts & I do not last I am impermanent in the name of Buddha meant to point out it's the same sleeve in an ancient poem she wept over and was inside of lasting meant that the one who was a kind of trope for the poem, the Genji of it, would never n'er be faithful meant to be faithful meant to be, couldn't but was ultimately faithful to himself to all of them himself the beauties the troubled ones of himself the awesome beauteous troubling ones of himself all tied in knots that nuptial means political but also under stars & placating doesn't necessarily mean that means attrition meant collusion means decision meant the disappointment of large sectors of grace meant she was fit to be tied meant she was not to be witched in her marriage trial meant that clouds would part the sea would part meant it was expected that one could be loved be wowed be vowed could be lamented meant the labels don't count they're all fraternizing fascinating with the enemy, what enemy? Say it, I do. I do what. Espouse.

— heuristically speaking

a long
  way
'round—
  "come"
says she
  —scarf on raven head—
it is my
tariqa
  my way
    (of prophet of dust)
& I inherit property of clan
  within the village
  or espouse
within
  other
Learned Families
& I will wed
(the way of my religion—)
choice—you see, said she
& among the shebab *who*
idle on the corner
    there's one with a secret
twist, head turned
  I have my eye on him
      that one

  no female sexuality
        outside the bonds of marriage
  (the real sheikh knows when I am pure
        or impure)

                    — god's hidden purpose

Love is a dram love is a cur love what makes the world go rue love is all there is & love how three times strange, love is stranger than even keel thinking. Once upon a time she was locked in the closet of her father's house & someone came calling. Knock three times. Stranger than a curtain. In one kingdom on the outskirts the curtain is made of light. Pull up your curtain lighthouse maiden. Even keel thinking is when you have the thoughts on straight up & up and you're able to do this with no disaster yet obstacles come like taboo & rant and yet you badly want to see the outside world. Knock three times. They try to lock you in & you seek a prince you seek an oftentimes cavalier. You badly want to see the finery & the young men of this world. And understand suffering & death. Boots of Lithuanian or Spanish leather. Or you want to go to the avant-garde movies. If you want to be alone you escape what is so familiar (*knock three times*). But die for love three times strange never. But that idea sounds its sound like qualifiers in the drama one dram of sex potion. Think it over. Drink up. Keel is fine in some neighborhoods some neck of woods & is a metaphor of getting to the sea now board & be a boat statue & boatwise tremble, but keel is real. It keels you over. She loosens the boat from its Lake District mooring but her lighthouse master has hidden the oars. She was always ever a romantic groomed on the gossamers of night & tide. Weight of a thousand kilos because life's like that a big burden. Once upon a time a lighthouse maiden walked these lands worrying her questions:

Question One: what's the meaning of an anchor?
Question Two: where is a lighthouse going in the future when you hear a film projector whirr with one lightbulb?
Three: do I need to be rescued?

Once upon a time the lighthouse keeper's daughter put a message half-joking in a bottle. *Don't marry me.* And the serpent of the sea came three times a challenge knocking on her window with his fine serpent head. And the third time she hid from the lighthouse lights that were binding themselves around her in the little tower, rings & rings of light, & she leapt forth into the sea. All to get away from the even keel loneliness but some say she jumped from the frying pan into the three times fire. Question Four: Is there an "e" in "dram"? or an extra "a" in "dram" or should I strike the "a" and replace it with a "u"? Once upon a time a sentence was diagrammed & there were a girl & a father both stranger than a curtain when a stranger arrives.

— *dram three times strange*

what is erroneous
is amorous

what excels its creation
is sound bites in a dream

what lover is so steady to stay by you
stays by you

what is the next way to get ballast on board duty free
maxim: spiritual baggage

spiritual love's an idea in most ceremonies
a kind footnote

and when I write "kind" I meant kind in the sense of children
for where else naturally does the contest of love but lie in kind?

in the genetic streams of children, *remember that,* in their genes

— *auguries*

Thinking you want to secure "on an even keel" is not enough in this bedroom. Curtains closed sheets are warm o yes you await "the touch." O yes it is the designated room where you lie prone. The bed is sound & made for ache & consummation of please marry this marrying feeling to the seduction of please marry this feeling to the desire of your head. Yet love is an enemy you need to get you off the track off back of possession & desire. Hear me out stake me now in the obligations of marrying love. Obsequies. How many years. Been to the desert (of love) lay down with scorpions mutated heat waves mirages old fellows of the carriage trade I tracked silk routes of abandon & commerce drunk on gold & other alchemical substances I fought the evil fight the desert fox the desert storm. I deserted my country for this one way out with sand way out with sand that blinds founded a kingdom there dreamed the enemy was the I I adjusted my psyche to locked to the pleasure of his company. It was a mitigated curse no it was blameless. If there ever was a good idea it was conceived in love, but a kind of paranoia sets in to make you think in reverse. Because love won't stop his whips was coming around with a harness on with a scorpion ready to sting. Stay the lashes love always brings bring them on of outrageous activity realms all the corners of the sensual universe. Because you want no one to touch you because you are the inexplicit virgin young & afraid. Steals your power. Or you might think that: hide from nuptials. And then be sacrificed the next day to a tuletary deity with your feather headdress on.

— *even keel*

rays
  of
broken
  /
  un
broken
light
    filter thru
    houses
  turned in
inaccessible
then
twisted on selves
    harsh orders of the old Imam
sacredness
  honor
integrity of women
  brokered
behind doors
  bottled up
go mad

where the Taliban rule

— anaclastic

Borrowed in blue. Rule & deal. What kinship system operative here if it be not language's spoon. A mouthpiece. Landfill's taboo, the jailhouse of diction. What jailhouse could hold the tribes together if it be not this psyche tried on for size. Words & costume. Measured in spoons like medicine. Dress me up like a bride. Minacious intercourse that old taboo. Dress me up like the mother of the bride. Try me on for size. Tie up my penis. Try me on for size & be & be how? Be in the jailhouse now. Try on a mother-of-the-bride psyche for size. Bush out in the bush now out in the bush they're spooning. And Mister's jailhouse now blasted with a crazy notion to go native, dress up native & confound you, confound myself, become the man-in-drag enemy. And make our taboo connection one of pride & innoculation it is preposterous they say this triage & wipe the blood from all the eyes-gone-bush shoulder & the arms-gone-bush shoulder & evasive animals-in-bush over the tops of trees gone bush & the trees here are butch & take that smirk off the face-gone-bush as your case may be.

— alien kinship says I was the
Trobriand islander

out of hand

careen
  singing I was
mutating down

being bad about to
  engage the horn
for me
   one time O

  cool night
flask at hip

   it might work for some this
    latch
this hitch
  this fix
  for others   they
run they run
  a deaf & dumb
  numb figure
 when we parted I lunged
   for safety
up the mountain
  & it's green green green
all the way down

                   — ***aries rising***

Say "bells" say "buckskin leggings" say "drumstick" say "domestic" say "throb" say "cautionary" say "quit it" say "I quit" say "I don't" say "gray sky, mountain shadow" say "men are working" say "women are sleeping" say "there are messages coming in" say "for you" say "there's so much to do" say "they want you doing a rhumba for the Chiapas benefit" say "I'll do it" "with a pretty dress (red) on" "we can wiggle our hips" she says & "catch a man." Say we can. "We can." Say "women come on weekends to give themselves to lovers" say "army camp" say "they married before he went to war" say "he died in war" say "she lived many years beyond" say "they were killed in the church," whole families say "they took out the men" in the other place. Say "Joan of Arc married to her faith" say "we are being tested." Say "many voices" say "many trials" say "polyphonic" say "human" say "the pathless forest" say "we enter the kinetic" "the virtual dumb-show" say "we go hand in hand."

— *rhumba*

if I was a carpenter
like the joke about the doctors
(everyone thinks the
doctor in the joke
is a man)
I
wouldn't marry
I'd have a baby
blind side anyway
    down by the old
broken down mill stream
(old girls labor too)

girls labor too
in invisible republics of
    murderous intent
a rational stoic
    presupposes that
you get down to
the rural side
                O momma!
& conceal the neolithic booty

  a child
if lucky
    comes out of a void
where birds are pronounced
    stange names
Falcon is one
Owl another
        & a sheriff looks the other way
in all the ballads he will kill her kill the child
maybe kill himself

stop this right now the cuckoo is a pretty bird
(augury & ceremony)
polly pretty polly come go along with me
before you get married some pleasure to see

      — selves the shelf of ballads made from

Chinese fireworks on the lawn. Lotus Opening in Distress to Love. Another Orgasm of Flower Mating Bee. You watch Thousands of Shattering Pavilions. You watch Sperm Rains Down Drips of the Pristine Maiden. Marriage ceremonies are milky ways, explosions programmed to go off & represent percussion at pure height of chaos. Thrum of heat & splendor of primordial form a blast a blast a blast a marriage happy archetype to war. Drink her Sweet Erotic Fountain. He is Salty Spray Come Down Again (One More Time). Thank the Warlords for Payday Sex. A Swell Way to Put Stars in the Sky. Rapture with a Purpose. Uptight Ministers of the Ancient Regime are Sputtering. Welcome Freedom of Firebrand Speech. Range to Knock off Enemies Within. Irony is a Loaded Gun. No More Tiananmen. No More Wage War with Neighbors in their Tibetan Monasteries. Tear Her Love Teat (Fragments of a Dream). The Tea Is Ready. Paper Tigers Will Have the Day with Grrr with Growl.

— *science annals*

as once one's flesh
never
    abandons
    its fastness—
it lives in
 Mina Loy's "wed/weld"
flexes toward
the room
fast again
    sculpted
or so
 Memling paints
—set on with
 cranial nerves—
the couple
    who settle
under spell of paint
  enchanted patrons
 in utterance
sepulchral
paint them
 funereal
encode them
  bow down ceremoniously
     old country
another's century's Adam & Eve
hinc ad horam *(encore)*
 hetero world
 hetero whirl

— spel

The bridegroom in ancient Sparta supped on the wedding night at the men's mess hall & visited his wife in the dark of night leaving her before daybreak. Children were born before the pair had seen each others' faces by day. Come hunt for me in the darkened room. In Morocco the bride's eyes are firmly closed. She is not allowed to open her eyes until she is set on the bridal bed. In Melanesia the bride is carried to her new home on someone's back wrapped in mats with palm fans held around her face because she is modest & shy. In Korea she must cover herself with long sleeves. Sight is a method of contagion. At Druse the bride is hidden in a long red veil. Umbrellas are connected with the sanctity of the head so let one be held over them. Association with women before you bed them will lead to effeminacy. Disguise is used as a concealment from danger (personal, spiritual, sexual) in the person of the other sex. A practice of Muslims in the northwest provinces of India recommends both bride & bridegroom wear dirty clothes for several days before the wedding. The head of a Kaffir bride is shaved. An old woman dresses up as a bride & dances before the assembled company. Amongst the Estonians the bride's brother dresses up in women's clothes & dances before the company. Create a marriage bower—arch of green bows. Build your canopy, O Jews. Substitute a mock bride for a real one. In Polonia a bearded man impersonates the bride. Among the Abyssinians when a princess is married she is accompanied by her sister dressed exactly like herself.

— *seclusion, concealment & veiling*

a bear destroys the dwarf & marries Snow White

through the hole in his coat Snow White thinks she sees
        the glittering of gold & thinks
it must be a hallucination
leave me alone dear children
dear Snow White & Rose Red
or you'll never wed if you act like this

Artemis of Brauron is your bear-goddess
supplicate her

(young girls of good families are given to the goddess
to serve from their twelfth to sixteenth year
they behave like tomboys—
don't wash speak roughly are called
bear cubs
then:
berserkers)

if they cannot contain themselves let them marry
for it is better to marry than be
aflame with passion (berserk)

later a king ordered silver hands to be made for his bride
fear of animal paws

— *silverhands*

Ditch a king marry another king. Switch a ring marry another ring. Eleanor of Aquitaine comes into inheritance in 1132 & holds on with rank & character. No *ius primae noctis* for her no serfdom for her under francophile stars under rank & file under the cloaks & daggers of arrogant byzantine doorways, a bridge, a tower, a fleeting glance a feckless handmaiden handed over to the king whoever he might be. An idiot? A tyrant? Puppet of state? Mere man with a grudge to grind down upon? Momentary specter thin shadow that flashes his wares (they were drygoods they were perishables) his wooden teeth that talk a line you fell for was he Sultan was he king really? Playboy likely or stevedore in disguise of a king. Pasha? Already a bunch of golden wives a bundle of nerves trying to get along neurological pathways haggling over shopping over circuits of desire & turn to dust. A pit a palace a corporate structure a Mercedes you escaped from & they all turn to dust. The day the buildings collapsed & many died the country got held hostage & turned to dust. The day the earth quaked in a hundred needy places. Back up a millennium. It is a mild night. How many crickets in a wedding night that is yours alone sweet sixteen. Nightingale come sing me here I'm sweet I'm sixteen. You imagine the sexual mind of a groom comes singing here for nubile sixteen. Is he pleased is he proud is he aroused you sleep with his cruel master? How many animals do you own really own or are you your father's forever sweet chattel? What is your remedy forever for undesired babes. Gather herbs of rosemary of rue of weed of nettle to dream sweet dreams put away babes in sleep put on your witchiest garb you are a changeling in any man's bed are you my wife you are not my wife he said & douses you with oil burns you to death you will never escape the stake you will be canonized in poetry you can cross over the moat now it's shadowy years ago you were bought & sold & died in a black rat plague.

— *ius primae noctis*

at the door dear marryings
at your chamber door
at the door clamorings
at your chamber door

let those who have wives live as if they had none!
clamor, clamor for love
I feel a divine pure bride to her his cunning Christ

thus Thecla a lovely young virgin renounced marriage
cut off her hair & dressed like a man
ran off to join the movement Jesus & Paul had initiated

lovely Mygdonia she became
to undo the sin of Adam & Eve

& among the names for marriage are
hitched, just married, tied the knot, gave over to a lord

— *divine jealousy*

For he must repair to his father-in-law, the meter-outer-of-support if this the male line continueth, in this it doth in all ways fair support its mastery (one supposes) & wise & fair continueth. For it will it must do this. Continueth. A desperate father sucks out the sperm of his dead son. Could the corpse of a woman be kept alive enough to bear a child is a question in America. This is a crazy way for lineage is nothing to fuss & tamper with about fairly. What up? Never wise enough she opines she fusses o never. He must walk on the bodies of those (this is Polynesia in another century) who celebrate for him this continuing of his the male line because if you are a father of a daughter you must have a son-in-law-to-profit & tell of & so be it the daughter consigns her nod as you age & never grow wiser. Would be enough to walk thus on all the bodies lined up door to door & why not touch the ground she menstruates upon. It is a human rug for kings who dare not walk upon their mothers for women are closer to the ground & must be avoided at all costs on this such a wild winsome wedding day. It is agreed upon in all the voices singing because it is custom & someone thought wide & colorful in its busyness, lying down of bodies, a sprawling carpet & colorful & how fast can you run it is a long way from his house to father-in-law's. And all manner of colored threads. Azure. Malachite. Gold. And a game. How fast you can sing & run how fast you sing & meet him along the way, he who is the chosen of her father somehow knowing this is his way. The way of his & his. You can sing for, game you can sing to. And women are fair game even if they can't play. They weave. Some say this is true in another century & one thinks of this & the parallel fractures of this century that ends that end & how to formulate new descriptions that it is the answer will be that it is always thus not that we can't have fun back then doing what we do in our very circumscribed streets of men & women "doings." Ways?

— street of human bodies

acts to father
further acts

image of the marrying maiden do prosper

— *China*

Promiscuity is not the same game plan resolving differences of desire. Does it ever & desire invariably furthers one. Suck him off in desire it furthers one. Be he here a snifter of rebellion be all of them furthering the path of least resistance. It furthers one. One doesn't lie back & smoulder links to repression & lack of desire. Desire to get him bedded wedded & with child is bettering one? You think nonsense. You think nonsense is an option that might be thinking itself a solution to nightly reruns demonic replays all night long do you take do you not take a pill for every stubborn obsolete thing he does & what about you the "she says she does" on top of that plus chemical hazard in the picture of a suburban backyard which nightly closes in on itself. More of California moving in. What is a neighborhood in the realm of desire with more of California moving in. When is your cancer turn? How will bodies ever free themselves of holy desire & fall in love again spilling over a modest page. It is an eclipse will do, a modest posture, maybe poetry one way to dream there are no enemies no beasties no sperm/egg banks online out to destroy the original self-made natural you. Never destroy one another in the drugs of life. Think magic of each other all my friends please all friends be kind. Where's promiscuity in the neighborhood these days. Go into town. The city is a stab in the back. What's the use. Read no burn your newspaper all the horrors of promiscuity & seduction. Tell me about it. On his side you have to give him credit for patience she's doing the dark deed somewhere after hours she's never there a mouth to feed. What about mouths to feed everywhere outside a rebellion sniff it out & suck them all off in their hunger trying to raid a pantry root through the trash bin one scam after another. This sentence gets dark it grows darker as the ruling class gets richer. He's just a deadbeat dad in this scenario spare him would you? Never.

— *abate the clause*

push the gesture

far as it will go

    & then
 claw
disjunction
  in her action

desire for another
  they say
  she, a Mrs, walked out one day to
  "see the animals in the zoo"
& never returns

                            — ***zoo***

If a man dies a bachelor the Balinese say that in the next life he will feed pigs. If a woman dies childless she is doomed to be suckled by a giant caterpillar. *Ngerorod* is the kind of wedding where the honeymoon preceeds the wedding ceremony. Friends of the suitor kidnap the woman in the fields on the road down by the river. She bites & kicks her abductors in mock self-defense. In these days she could be whisked away in a hired sedan. The couple repairs to a friend's house stocked with provisions, offerings, the woman's wardrobe. The woman's father sounds the alarm! What has become of his daughter? A research party is organized which returns unsuccessful, exhausted. The couple must consummate their marriage before special offerings (*sesayut tabuh rah*) wilt. Emissaries of the groom visit the bride's father to argue the benefits of the union. The father gives in after a suitable bride price has been agreed upon. The groom's father must finance the wedding. The actual wedding is forty-two days after staged kidnapping. They are, however, already married in the eyes of god. *Mapadik* is marriage by consent. Polygamy is quite rare. At one time the wife of a prince could hold varying levels of status in a *puri*, depending on caste & whether she ranked as first, second, third, or fourth wife. The prince did not even appear at his wedding ceremony with a low-caste bride. She was ceremonially married to his *kris*, or a tree. A woman may divorce by simply leaving home if he is cruel under an occult power or impotent.

— *wilt*

of coupling
　　cost toward a
　　　　cost un
coupled
as alimony sings
& cutlery rises

　　storm-spoons?

dishes for asking
　　& cost goes down

in presence of taxing

tax-spoons?

　　　cup won't run
in a child's line
　　except lively strut
　　　　on earth

lines of resistance tally
　　she wants a body next-to-her
back
& be her baby

thinking: grass blade grass blade
　　he's got a mind, my son, sharp as that

cunieform
crosses
out
infraction

that couples go free
goods tallied
a second best bed

human agents
—widows or widowers—
stories bind them in a past

never get your due,
one dies yet
her drama not over
there's one more chorus
antique prop
a fan   an exorcism
your stage paint runs
you take up a sorrowful drum
or a lamp to signify night
the Noh tells us
to be
married once
in ancient urgency
ghosts speak of this &
pound a log
that
a true lover demonized
marries for eternity

— *divertere (ghost)*

Bought big red wooden hoop bracelets about eight-inch diameter. Hung them on sad potted tree (eight feet high) on a little side portico. Four bracelets? Picked up in side market along with incense. Brahmin asked if we had any children. We stumbled out "No" meaning not together. He recited a prayer/chant, hung up the bracelets (had us hang them) on tree, and said "now you will." We always thought of it as our marriage. We always thought of it as a link to pandemonium to a spring festival with bonfires blazing everyone bring their offering to burn their ropes their old rags to burn to the cowherder's song to the king of Holi riding backward on a donkey to goats' bleaching bones to fluting Lord Krishna with a garland of old shoes 'round his neck to world destruction to world purification where the ravisher is acting ravished & wives laud it over their husbands & everything moves upsidedown in a twilight world in a topsy turvy world. *Sandhyabasha.* We always thought we could go back to the Golden Age of Truth, the *satya yuga* where persons knew neither illness nor want & lived for thousands of years simple virtuous innocent before greed before private property & everyone is hoarding acquisitions before life spans grow short & war disease & poverty come in. Pilgrimage & lunar rites we partake of & cult spots both savage & sanctified where the word color means "red" it is the only color, color: blood. We go there. We thought we go there of primeval Fish Tortoise & Boar who become our deities we thought we go there of monkey-faced Hanuman & Vishnu asleep upon the canopied Cobra waters. I was Durga-Parvati to your Siva—milky Laksmi to your Vishnu. Our children are magic bracelets we hang these old concentric lives we go there upon & we always thought of it as our time our bond our duty our right to be witnessed in front of bloodthirsty Kali Calcutta's queen maddened with earthly/unearthly desire.

— *Kaligat*

sutee
  a suture
a susurration
    crimson

some skull broke apart
  started up as if to speak—
tongue of ash

mantra ascends with
  plume of smoke

  throw herself—all in gauzy white—
on the flaming corpse

              — burning ghat

Sounds improbable but one day coyote went along the human road & spotted a human woman with a cheeky look. How about it? About what? About the look you have. You want some trouble mister dog? Ho she was cheeky all right. You want to see the insides of my wagon? (She was of the tribe of Roma he thought or something.) Ok ok, what'll it take? Will you take off those fancy frilly clothes? Just as you say, my pet. Will you dance a jig? Just as you say. Will you do the deed? First you sign here (*she reads*) *lawful, spectacular, I'm the wife to be true & faithful to* . . . She was guiding him inside the ramshackle wagon & you put that love instrument in this handsome box, my pet. She knew if she took the orneriness out of coyote she'd have some animal powers. She came at him with scissors that'd been concealed in a glistening shawl o no o no you don't he barks & grabs her cheeky look for his own power-box & goes on his way away from her naked face way off the human road.

— *coyote almost takes a wife*

it was
a force
  a living
force
  I was hit
that hard
by what
    I
saw

(this is so good you
wouldn't know it
was painted by a woman)

        Krasner's painterly
identity in
Pollock's absence

                — **metabolic**

She alone in her sprint of him alone in her welcomed & wedded carnal sense of him this is holy holy this is holy she in fierce love of him tender like her son she would have by him the need to make it holy make this holy side by side in the holy bed & placement of him in her is holy & what wonders of love & a child & of partners in the mysteries of love that take a testament to the wedded gaze of owning him how fierce he is mine he is holy. Gaze long into him how holy he is watch him move around how holy. Watch & wake the flesh to be holy. For he is the comely yearned for partner in the wedded light of holiness binding the thread that runs through the holy beads is holy. It is a clear thread. It is liquid. It is silver. It is gold. It is holy.

— *alone in her sprint of him*

the world may be shaped as nourished
like flowers nourished
inside the world named as people nourished

two of them

the way snakes leave their skins behind
two of them are people
& they might long hours being people
    think on this becoming other
        than what they were once
& dress as Other Snakeskins
& let them as couple be spared their original skin
which was young thin tender
& be as metaphors representing themselves
to themselves beyond themselves
in the house of themselves
a single rose might stand in for this couple
shed a petal, disappear

— **thin-skinned**

I do yes I do I promise to love & placate Mister/Mrs in times of trial and propitiate the gods of language if they exist & sometimes I would doubt this of marriage obey yes I do I promise to trust the stairs we daily climb to trust the floor we'll walk on putting heavier objects than ourselves upon & yes I do promise to be beautiful to be the arranger of the *domus* hold a mirror up to nature in all I arrange & to love and obey the walls the ceiling the bed the shelves & take care of Mister/Mrs in sickness the shock of & wearying & destabilization of & there will always be sickness & will not force any rooms any nouns to weep any things to weep I will be the epitome of domesticity in the arrangements & maintenance of material stuff & I will not weep I will walk I will walk with you & I will I will stumble with you about the things the nouns of the house. And even if the verbs rise up the nouns our bullies will not fail us & we will be straddled with our debt to them. The objects they become will weigh us down & yet we will stumble together about the stones about the nouns of the house.

— *nouns of the house*

& smash a glass

I smash the glass

O smash the glass

I enter the tent & smash the glass
  & smash a glass I smash the glass

break the seal & smash the glass
  & smash a glass I smash the glass

& smash the glass
  I smash the glass
& smash a glass
  O smash the glass

— *glass hymen rite*

Mister a bold apostrophe an article to do bidding of an astonishment a tremor Mister was a tragi–comedy. Allegorical is the stance of Mister as a statement is a father & blunt speech a tyranny pitching a curve entering the back streets of Denver. Dad, Dad is the call. Dad Dad an essential ingredient to frame a blind spot to waltz towards. A building code will charm the Mrs maybe only maybe & her blue chips will be up. She & all applaud a Nasdaq jump. And would not rig a poll for her case for she is independence itself flaring & flaming & flaming in noonday sun. Suspect a provocation in the cease-fire deal expect the *joglaresa* to sing her song for supper for mouths to feed logging on into future duty, future duty the laws do tighten their claws upon.

— *future duty*

man's eros seems
      a boon to act upon

comes home & is
kind Dad
& this is true boon

"Dad" the image of
true one,
who sings rakes & slays
      the dragon daily

 nightly guess
it's up to others
  to call down a story

forced migration
poverty
genocide

blanch without fear
  it's just crazy love
they have for each other

it's on the news to rally for

"faith" is the quintessential story

& her children are
  Sun & Moon

or Day & Dawn

when star gazers once
had fantasies &
were able to function

in a full swing of paradise

& command a settled fertile house

*— **fertile house***

Image of tall bed. Grow weak. Groan. Her cliché. Her Japanese robe. Her French makeup. His Italian shampoo. His Mexican codeine. Her frugal meal. His tender sport. His handy tenspot. Her black spaghetti straps. Her balanced forms. His normal accent her prance his ancient sea route. Her favorite spot his forgivable lapses. Her lapses. Her dogged pursuit. His emotional blackmail. Her cajolement. Her brow. Her swift retreat. His favorite shrine. Her dusky body. His entanglement. A cushion. His entanglement. Her dispossession. Her deposition. His reply. His gaze. Her window. Her patterned negligee. His lasting impression. Her accelerated rhythm. His slow thrust. Her cry. His anguish. His edit. Her speech. His reply. Her decency. Her tyranny. Her edit. His scope. Her tempo. Her silence. Her mind is now wandering. Her jargon. His episodes. Her rapture. Her cry. His cry her anguish. Her labor of love. Her jewels. Her juice her rings. His anarchy. Her solace. Her delight. Her come on his taut muscle. Her deleterious purity. His stamina. Her sweet scent. Her yet his excitement. His yet her quickened breath. His heave. His yet her nakedness. His ascent. His rasp. Her cry. Her scent. Their rub. Rivulets of semen. Yet he of her notion is spent in her terror. Her yet his look of abominable passion is his notion of how her terror is spent. Yet she of his notion is not spent in his terror of her. Her cry. Her rupture to him. His feel. Her look in his eye. Contorted face. He says look at me. His fist open now. His gentleness. Her heat yet it belongs to him. His closed eye. Her struggle. Her glimpse on his struggle yet on her own. Her chill at him yet his repair. Her wounded thought although it might yet be joy. Her sure joy. Her sure wet thigh. Her damp cloth he yet fetches for her.

— *her sure joy*

adultery
　is old-fashioned
pool-shimmer
　on the surface they rise
embrace me in couple
　I said nothing but rising
stay locked
　I saw these three—
the she
　the philodendron
& the husband
this is his way
　imagine a hotel
imagine a two-piece suit
　& turquoise bra of her suit
float near them
　piece of hammered silver
then silk chemise
　smug smile it is in ink
　she was maybe widow's peak
I float over
　they log miles
flash blind smiles
little darling little darling
& slowly sink　very slim
but I am small
　lover in the world
in the small world widening
　spoke between them
accost her there's public room
　a halted space
where a bookstore man sees
　he could always see

say what they had to
  it was I, a wife
was something to read
  mattress & younger
with a veteran hand
  so how complain
like she was jewelry said
  you didn't know?
you out of them all didn't
didn't know?
shock like death
  I was submerged
& she a red light
  go go
under her excitement
  modern or strong
change all of these things
  I want to
but back to bed now
  in headache
slow revival
  think everyone's been
on every
  side of every old situation
remember
  & he all over the bed once
far from wifey
  & me the red light
go go

— *adultery*

Yearning in his voice man to man man on man had remembered I only wash dishes & laughed man to man was like in pictures you make a case take a stand for the benefits of survival's kind palimony. He is gentlemanly young erudite discreet they are friends & flirting amours dear marriage come later. A maestro gaze, he makes dances, he shoots ambulatory films, had remembered & said now it is final now, a final illness, shifts from man to man in this culture so let's marry before it gets late. Overstuffed ready chair opera gloves paperwork footlocker, a carriage trade stands for myths together. Postcards from Berlin or the jewelbox theater La Fenice in Venezia where you in marriage watched Figaro burnt down. He dies he wishes on the Metropolitan Opera steps. One last diva stand. And when you just say opera how trivializing it gets what opera. It was *Pelleas et Melisande* of Debussy. What man what death what couple. His name in subtext is Warren. Crawled down there someone said who loves him like that he was mad for the place & music ringing always in an ear. Strauss is a favorite or maybe it's the aria from the one when the woman was a man maybe Strauss again. And Lucia Lamermoor someone said was one of mine was what he said.

And after this man is gone try the different heartbreak tones of Saigon.

— male gaze male

—a radiant primordial music
—I can still hear it
—all but dying into love
—that too
—inside it's table linen, candles, you know . . .
—amenities, amiabilities
—but deeper than that it germinates
—you mean never giving up on each other?
—sometimes . . .
—ancient vestiges, saintly, sparse?
—more connected to nature, like that
—a simultaneous response
—yes
—gregarious movements as in a duet
—will it cure? That's the mighty thing
—yes

—cure

Four sopranos one mezzo two tenors one baritone three bass sing into the last watershed of Mozart's career. "Cinque dieci": the engaged couple, servants of the house, are measuring the room and trying on a hat for the wedding. The count renounces his *droit de Seigneur* but still has designs on Susanna. Opera *buffa* one crazy day. He Figaro has borrowed money from Marcellina & has agreed to marry her if he defaults. The count is heard approaching: Susanna hides Cherubino behind a chair etcetera. Figaro protests he cannot marry Marcellina without his parents' consent. When he discovers the birthmark on his arm it seems he is actually the lost son of Marcellina. How can he marry his own mother? *The garden at night:* Barbarina the go-between has lost a pin. Figaro concludes Susanna is unfaithful Marcellina warns Susanna we women should stick together ("Il capro e la capretta.") Barbarino is preparing to meet Cherubino in a pavilion. Figaro summons Basilio and Bartolo to witness the betrayal. Basilio moralizes about the wisdom of not resisting one's superiors adding a tale of his own hot wild youth. Figaro's monologue (obbligato recitative and aria, "Aprite un po' quegl'occhi") uses raw gestures to convey the terrors of sexual betrayal. Horn fanfares mock him without mercy. He overhears but cannot see his beloved Susanna who is disguised as the countess & who is aware of his presence. She confides her amorous longings to the night. The characters mistake identities blunder in the dark receive kisses & blows intended for others. Cherubino begs the disguised "Susanna" (actually the countess) for a kiss. The count begins to woo "Susanna" who responds shyly. Figaro expresses impotent rage. As the key changes from G to E♭ a serenade-like melody evokes the bizarre "peace" of the night. Where are we? The suburbs? Seeing the "countess" (Susanna) Figaro tells her what is going on, although recognizing her by her voice he nevertheless pays the "countess" passionate court. Susanna boxes his ears again, enraged. He is ecstatically happy with this response from his fiancée. The duo enacts a passionate scene: Figaro pleading love to the "countess," on cue with an abrupt key change (B♭ to G). The count bursts in calling witnesses

rousing the whole neighborhood & universe dragging everyone in-
cluding the false countess from the pavilion shouting accusations. He
denounces her refuses forgiveness while the real countess stands in
Susanna's humble clothes. Everyone is stunned. The humbled count
realizes his mistake begs for forgiveness receives her radiant response
which builds into a blissful hymn. The curtain comes down on one
dysfunctional day.

— *le nozze, a romp*

North American French,
from French bardache,
catamite, *from Italian*
    dialectical bardasia,
from Arabic bardaj, *slave,*
from Persian bardah, *prisoner,*
from Middle Persian vartak,
from Old Iranian varta

cross

  the gender

    barrier

all my languages

with

  skirt & bangle
she cautions

more verbs! verbs!
to get a husband

                — berdache

Something amiss awry the whole community knows it. An ill-starred conjunct. Adjacent distress. The village is a weather system. The villagers a hotline. He buries his wife under the floorboards & takes a mistress. She takes up with a mere child & wears vermillion on her wedding day. He brings in a foreigner who doesn't pass muster with the village elders. There's old clan revenge on the intruder's head. Disparity in the ages of the spouses. Sixty to twenty, twelve to fifty & so on. The merry widower takes a blue-haired wife. Husbands are beaten with wooden spoons by their women. Girls turn up their noses at suitors of high repute & pick those richer too old and/or foreign. Girls lead a dissolute life drinking & whoring on the outskirts of same village. Pregnant fiancées marry boldly in pristine white. A youth sells himself to a woman for money puts on her clothes struts in the doorway & then sells himself to a man. An overly married woman brazenly commits adultery. A girl takes a married man as lover pretends to be his sister at the fancy hotel. A large crowd makes a din to frighten away an eclipse one sultry night in Minnesota & many windows get smashed at the fancy hotel. A syntagmic sequence gets broken & all hell breaks loose. Charivari punishes reprehensible unions. Charivari rules.

— *charivari/syntagma*

                    friendship
for beings
   all guises
      tender as when
  Krishna dresses as milkmaid

milks the cows with his beloveds

him in the adventure of it

old animisms
ply
  atavistic runes

Praxitilean curve of the blue god's hips
    outside cyberspace

            — outside cyberspace

On the day of his death he stopped work and turned to Catherine who was in tears "Stay Kate, keep just as you are—I will draw your portrait—for you have ever been an angel to me." As he finished he put it down & began to sing verses & hymns. "My beloved, they are not mine." William Blake was singing out of gladness. Right before their forty-fifth anniversary he told his wife they would never be parted that he would be close with her always. At six in the evening he breathed his last "like the sighing of a gentle breeze." "His eye Brighten'd and He burst out into Singing the things he saw in heaven." She then saw him continually when he used to come and sit with her for two or three hours every day. He took his chair & talked to her just as he would have done had he been alive. William, sweet William. On the day of her death she was as calm & as cheerful as her husband had been "repeating texts of scripture and calling continually to her William, as if he were only in the next room, to say she was coming to him, and would not be long now."

— the marriage of William Blake

night's oral
  death rattle

erosion

attrition

  see an invented person

holy broth of marriage

inverted
        a human dreams as one
  choral level
many voices

    showers of stars
clouds
 flames
    a-spin

for it comes to this: death as coda
& marriage kind sentence of death
    a work of life of art of love 'til death
  & though you might eschew
you & you & one & one
  long years'   flesh & stories
grown old in it singing
    out of the prison
  into
language's allegorical dream

— *allegorical dream*

Thy lip thy eye thy brow thy single nature thy chorus thy marriage to chastity thy kind office for me thy supreme throne thy corruption thy taxes thy fantasies thou taper's light thy chime thy soft bed thy beauteous state thy phoenix thy lark thy vain search thy black wings thy shibboleths thy lust thy list againe thy tears they are women at sea thy babes at suckle thy ingenuity in composition thy traitorous song thy civility thy wounds wound round again thy affections thy words & dust thy moist lament thy divorced soul thy dirge thy lament thy weeping verse thy weary hours thy exile thy ashy shroud thy amp thy steed thy lamb thy earthly ball a coin thy torrid zone thy pain thy calme estate thy persuasions thy sickle thy marigold thy polygamy aye thy shell of sinne thy chaste flesh crumbles to dust thy eaglet thy din thy sex & place thy taper thy puling poet whose griefe is a puddle thy wounds flames darts orient deep thy fading rose thy spicy nest thy fragrant bosome thy noisome plant whose perfume does utter "thy" thy mortall beauty thy waving sea thy Mermaid's croon amid the dunes thy high Palace thy Alchemie thy Copper Mine thy glow-worme thy Aethiop bride thy farre-stretched powre that overrides thy hill of ice thy selfe accurst thy cloathes thy jest thy melancholy eye thy Tissues stalkt their high rays balk thy altar's smoake thy Hermits of discretion thy starry jewel thy curtains fair damask thy shade where lovers lie in progression thy marriage vow thy vow undone thy privation thy small star thy drouzy head thy flowry prime thy veines shot thy lovely Rose ere going thy Apologie thy delicious cup thy cup is strong thy cup divine little drops of dew thy cup emptied thy troops thy downy wings thy woman cup & cunt forebear thy golden clime in ev'ry aire thy man's pride & steed thy walled Towne thy dozen's dozen thy pitty thy Angells voyce thy humble chill thy grave is frozen thy herbes & flow'res thy active Star thy fork'd lightning thy deepest scar thy anxious care thy pavaillion in baths do steepe them in common marriage amen.

— *thy lip*

thy lip againe   thy firm seal
in endlesse complexity
to read between
  fault lines
of prose's
poetry
  or gender blurred
in calm distinction
  'tween mates of
    a mated game
for artist is kind mate
to all grammar
all
decipherable patterns
(see them see them in their glory)
  sexual potencies
social conflicts
economies
histories
        civilization's orthodoxies
        oppositional antics
          that muster
in wicked harmony
  & I do take this vow in meditation
that marriage be spontaneous vision
  beyond thought or speech
  outed
    in sentenc'd incision

                              — coda a code

ABOUT THE AUTHOR

Anne Waldman grew up on Macdougal Street in New York City, grad-
uated from Bennington College, was an assistant director and director of
the seminal Poetry Project at St. Mark's-in-the-Bowery Church from
1966 to 1978, founded (with Allen Ginsberg) the Jack Kerouac School
of Disembodied Poetics at the Naropa Institute in Boulder, Colorado, in
1974, has published more than thirty pamphlets and books of poetry,
edited Angel Hair Magazine & Books (with Lewis Warsh), Full Court
Press (with Ron Padgett & Joan Simon), Rocky Ledge Cottage Edi-
tions and Magazine (with Reed Bye), and has edited three anthologies
of writing from the Poetry Project, including *Out of This World*
(Crown/Random House, 1992). She has also edited *Nice to See You:
Homage to Ted Berrigan,* and *Disembodied Poetics: Annals of the Jack Kerouac
School,* with Andrew Schelling (University of New Mexico Press, 1994)
and *The Beat Book.* She has collaborated with a range of artists, including
Elizabeth Murray, Red Grooms, Yvonne Jacquette, Joe Brainard, Susan
Rothenberg, Richard Tuttle, and George Schneeman. A celebrated
"performance poet," she works extensively with dancers and musicians.
She has performed her work in India, Central and South America, Ger-
many, Holland, the Czech Republic, and England, as well as across the
United States and Canada. She has made numerous recordings and
videotapes, including *Uh-oh Plutonium!, Eyes in All Heads, Live at
Naropa,* and *Battle of the Bards.* She has taught at the New College of
California, Stevens Institute of Technology, and the Institute of Ameri-
can Indian Arts in Santa Fe. She is on the faculty of the Schule für Dich-
tung in Vienna. She is a distinguished Professor of Poetics at the Naropa
University and curriculum director of the annual Summer Writing Pro-
gram. She is two-time winner of the Heavyweight Championship Po-
etry Bout in Taos, New Mexico. A practicing Buddhist and "magpie
scholar," she has lived and traveled for periods in India and Bali. She was
the recipient of the Shelley award for poetry in 1996.

Ted Berrigan	*Selected Poems*
Philip Booth	*Pairs*
Jim Carroll	*Fear of Dreaming*
Jim Carroll	*Void of Course*
Nicholas Christopher	*5° & Other Poems*
Carl Dennis	*Ranking the Wishes*
Diane di Prima	*Loba*
Stuart Dischell	*Evenings and Avenues*
Stephen Dobyns	*Common Carnage*
Stephen Dobyns	*Pallbearers Envying the One Who Rides*
Paul Durcan	*A Snail in My Prime*
Amy Gerstler	*Crown of Weeds*
Amy Gerstler	*Nerve Storm*
Debora Greger	*Desert Fathers, Uranium Daughters*
Robert Hunter	*Glass Lunch*
Robert Hunter	*Sentinel*
Barbara Jordan	*Trace Elements*
Jack Kerouac	*Book of Blues*
Ann Lauterbach	*And For Example*
Ann Lauterbach	*On a Stair*
William Logan	*Night Battle*
William Logan	*Vain Empires*
Derek Mahon	*Selected Poems*
Michael McClure	*Huge Dreams: San Francisco and Beat Poems*
Michael McClure	*Three Poems*
Carol Muske	*An Octave Above Thunder*
Alice Notley	*The Descent of Alette*
Alice Notley	*Mysteries of Small Houses*
Lawrence Raab	*The Probable World*
Anne Waldman	*Kill or Cure*
Anne Waldman	*Marriage: A Sentence*
Rachel Wetzsteon	*Home and Away*
Philip Whalen	*Overtime: Selected Poems*
Robert Wrigley	*In the Bank of Beautiful Sins*
Robert Wrigley	*Reign of Snakes*